NASCAR Behind the Scenes

Matt Doeden
AR B.L.: 3.0
Points: 0.5   MG

The World of NASCAR

NASCAR
Behind the Scenes

by Matt Doeden

Reading Consultant:
Barbara J. Fox
Reading Specialist
North Carolina State University

Content Consultant:
Betty L. Carlan
Research Librarian
International Motorsports Hall of Fame
Talladega, Alabama

Capstone

Mankato, Minnesota

Blazers is published by Capstone Press,
151 Good Counsel Drive, P.O. Box 669, Mankato, Minnesota 56002.
www.capstonepress.com

Library of Congress Cataloging-in-Publication Data
Doeden, Matt.
    NASCAR behind the scenes / by Matt Doeden.
    p. cm. — (Blazers. The World of NASCAR)
    Includes bibliographical references and index.
    ISBN-13: 978-1-4296-1283-8 (hardcover)
    ISBN-10: 1-4296-1283-5 (hardcover)
    1. NASCAR (Association) — Juvenile literature. 2. Stock car racing —
United States — Juvenile literature. I. Title. II. Series.
GV1029.9.S74H37 2008
796.72 — dc22   2007029963

Summary: Describes what goes on behind the scenes in the sport of NASCAR
    racing, including how pit crews build, repair, and improve race vehicles.

Essential content terms are **bold** and are defined on the spread where they
first appear.

Editorial Credits
Tom Adamson & Mandy Robbins, editors, Bobbi J. Wyss, designer; Jo Miller,
    photo researcher

Photo Credits
AP Images/Chris Garnder, 6–7; Chuck Burton, 12–13; Ric Feld, cover;
    Terry Renna, 8
Corbis/GT Images/George Tiedemann, 28–29
Getty Images for NASCAR/Chris Trotman, 24; Rusty Jarrett, 18–19;
    Streeter Lecka, 15; Getty Images, Inc./ Darrell Ingham, 17; Nick Laham, 9
The Sharpe Image/Sam Sharpe, 5, 10, 14, 20, 22–23, 27

1 2 3 4 5 6 13 12 11 10 09 08

Table of Contents

In the Garage

The garage buzzes with activity. It's the night before the race. During practice, the car's engine blew up. The crew team scrambles to repair the damage.

The team pounds out dents. They put in a backup engine. Team members carefully connect all of the engine's hoses and wires.

TRACK FACT!

NASCAR crew teams use wind tunnels and computers to show how the car cuts through the air.

After a long night of work, the car is ready. The crew rolls it out to the track.

The crowd cheers for the driver.
But few fans are aware of the crew
that made the car ready to race.

From the Ground Up

Most fans know very little about the workers who build race cars. The garage area is filled with team members making **adjustments** to each car.

adjustment — a minor change that improves a car's performance

Car of Tomorrow frame

NASCAR teams build their cars from scratch. First, the team carefully welds together steel rods. These rods make up the *frame*.

frame — welded metal that forms the main shape of a race car

Team members called fabricators shape the car's body panels. These sheets of metal fit over the *chassis*. The metal forms the body of the car.

chassis — the frame, wheels, and machinery that support a car's body

TRACK FACT!

NASCAR has strict rules about how cars must be shaped.

Under the Hood

NASCAR teams also work on the engine. Race cars have big engines. They push cars to 200 miles (322 kilometers) per hour.

TRACK FACT!

Racing is hard on an engine. Teams build a new engine for each race.

Teams put in different *gears* at
different race tracks. For short tracks,
the gears allow the car to speed up quickly.
For long tracks, gears maintain high speeds.

gear — one of a set of wheels with teeth that fit together to affect the movement of a machine

Final Touches

Before each race, teams set up the car's *suspension system*. The driver tests the car. He tells the team how to make it handle better.

suspension system — springs and shock absorbers that smooth out a car's up-and-down movements

Teams decide how much air to put in the tires. They stack the tires neatly near the team's pit box.

During a race, the garage teams often beat out dents from crashes or replace parts that have broken during the race.

Jimmie Johnson and crew chief Chad Knaus

The team's crew chief watches over all of the work. The driver tells the crew chief how the car should be set up. They also talk about race *strategy*.

strategy — a plan for winning the race

The team works hard until the car is ready to race. After the race, they head back to the garage to start all over again.

The Hauler

The driver of a team's car gets all of the attention. But every NASCAR team has another driver that fans never hear about. This team member drives a big hauler.

Teams move cars and equipment from track to track in the hauler. Race teams load the hauler right after a race ends. Hauler drivers often have to drive across the country in only a couple of days.

Glossary

adjustment (uh-JUHST-muhnt) — a slight change made to improve a car's performance

body panels (BAH-dee PAN-uhls) — pieces of metal that make up the outside frame of a vehicle

chassis (CHA-see) — the frame, wheels, axles, and parts that hold the engine of a car

frame (FRAYM) — a structure that shapes and supports something

gear (GEER) — one of a set of wheels with teeth that fit together; gears move in circles to run machines.

pit box (PIT BOX) — the small area on pit row where a team changes a car's tires, adds fuel, and makes minor adjustments

strategy (STRAT-uh-jee) — a plan for winning a race

suspension system (suh-SPEN-shuhn SISS-tuhm) — a system of springs and shock absorbers connecting the main body of a car to the wheels and axles

Read More

Barber, Phil. *From Finish to Start: a Week in the Life of a NASCAR Racing Team.* The World of NASCAR. Chanhassen, Minn.: Child's World, 2004.

Buckley, James. *Life in the Pits: Twenty Seconds that Make the Difference.* The World of NASCAR. Excelsior, Minn.: Tradition Books, 2003.

Doeden, Matt. *Under the Hood.* NASCAR Racing. Mankato, Minn.: Capstone Press, 2008.

Internet Sites

FactHound offers a safe, fun way to find Internet sites related to this book. All of the sites on FactHound have been researched by our staff.

Here's how:
1. Visit *www.facthound.com*
2. Choose your grade level.
3. Type in this book ID **1429612835** for age-appropriate sites. You may also browse subjects by clicking on letters, or by clicking on pictures and words.
4. Click on the **Fetch It** button.

FactHound will fetch the best sites for you!